Ella the El

Educating Children about Asthma

Shelly Weiss
Ed.S, LMHC, CRC
Illustrated by Christopher Harmon

Childswork Childsplay.com
CALL 1•800•962•1141

A Brand of The Guidance Group
www.ChildsworkChildsplay.com

Ella the Elephant: Educating Children about Asthma
© 2013 Shelly Weiss Ed.S, LMHC, CRC
Published by Childswork/Childsplay
A Brand of The Guidance Group
1-800-962-1141
www.ChildsworkChildsplay.com

All rights reserved.

ISBN: 978-1-58815-194-0

No part of this book may be reproduced or transmitted in any form or by any means, electronic or mechanical, including photocopying, recording, or by any information storage and retrieval system without written permission from the publisher.

Printed in the United States of America.

The stories and opinions expressed herein are solely those of the author. We do not attempt to give medical advice but address the emotional health of the subject based on best psychological practices. Please consult a medical professional with your questions and concerns.

INTRODUCTION

Dear Readers,

My name is Shelly and I was born different from most babies; I was born with cerebral palsy. My speech is slurred and I have a crooked walk because of the cerebral palsy. I wrote this book to help others understand that the world is full of people who have various medical conditions, gifts, talents, personalities, and appearances. Ella is a character who, despite various challenges, maintains a positive attitude and stays determined through it all! I hope you enjoy Ella's story.

Your Friend,
Shelly

Ella the Elephant has trouble breathing,
when she runs or plays, she ends up wheezing.

She has to stop and gasp for air.
Each time it happens, it's quite a scare!

Catching her breath becomes so tough,
she has to calm down from gasping so much.

Asthma tightens her chest within.
An inhaler helps her breathe again.

The doctor gives her lots of lung tests
to help make sure her treatment is best.

Blowing air in a tube is a test that she tries.
When her asthma's bad, the ball doesn't rise.

What causes her attacks when she's gasping for air?
Concerns such as this the doctor answers with care.

She may outgrow asthma when she ages,
or the asthma may go through different stages.

Since the doctor explained why her chest tightens,
when she has an attack, she no longer gets frightened.

Either way, Ella has it under control,
she takes her inhaler wherever she goes.

She rests when she's tired and always acts smart,
by taking her doctor's asthma rules to heart.

Ella runs lots of races, competing a lot,
refusing to be limited by the condition she's got.

Discussion questions for the child who has asthma:

1. How do you feel about having asthma?
2. What's the hardest thing about making new friends?
3. What would you tell people about yourself that you think they do not know?
4. Are you treated differently at home because you have asthma? At school? If so, how? How does that make you feel?
5. What is your favorite thing about the character in this book?

Discussion questions for the child who does not have asthma:

1. How do you feel when you see someone who has asthma?
2. Have you ever known or do you know someone who has asthma? If so, what was/is that experience like?
3. What can you learn from people who have asthma?
4. What questions do you have about people who have asthma?
5. What is your favorite thing about the character in this book?

NOTE: All questions should be reviewed before use. All questions may not be appropriate for every child and one should use their discretion as to which questions are appropriate to use.